Dirt Road Doctorate

**10 PRINCIPLES FOR BUSINESS SUCCESS
FROM THE SCHOOL OF BUSTED KNUCKLES**

BY GARY GALE NORRIS

Dirt Road Doctorate:
10 Principles for Business Success from the School of Busted Knuckles

© 2017 Gary Gale Norris

All rights reserved. No part of this book may be reproduced, distributed, or transmitted in any form or by any means, including photocopying, recording, or other electronic or mechanical methods without prior written permission of the publisher or author. Except in the case of commercial uses permitted by copyright law. For permission request write and/or email to the publisher (Gary Gale Norris) addressed "Attention Permissions" to the following email address: gary.norrisventures@gmail.com.

ISBN-13: 978-1542662123

First Printing, 2017

Book Design and Illustrations by Navah Studios

Printed by CreateSpace, An Amazon.com Company
PRINTED IN THE UNITED STATES OF AMERICA

Dedication

First, to my heavenly Father. Your grace and mercy for me have been infinite. I have single-handedly attempted to exhaust Your vast supply of each for me. The truth that You love me with all my mess and have never withheld Your love from me calls me to offer the same to others. Thank you, Father.

To my Hero, the strongest man I have ever known: my dad. I love you with a fervor and depth that only eternity will reveal. I will never get over who you are. I am the man I am today because of you. Dad, you have always been, and always will be my hero. Thank you for loving me no matter what and pointing me to God by the way you love me.

To the greatest and sweetest and strongest mom. Your compassion to everyone around you and your uncanny knowledge of medical application when no doctor was close is epic. You too have pointed me to our Lord my whole life. I will never get over our moments of transparency and the bleak hours when the only light to me was your voice. Thank you for being brave enough to carry light to me. I love you, Mama.

To my brother. You are also as strong as those trees we used to ride together. You are closer to me than a brother. You are my dearest friend who shared bumps and bruises. Tears and laughter. You are my blood and I will defend you to the death. There is no one who holds your place in my life. You will always be my brother. My friend. My defender. And yes….you will always be navel lint. Jus' sayin. I love you, Brother.

DIRT ROAD DOCTORATE

Table of Contents

Chapter 1   Cap Guns and Gas Tanks..................1

Chapter 2   Check the Vine....................7

Chapter 3   Equal Opportunity Quarterback........13

Chapter 4   "Never Learn No Younger"................19

Chapter 5   Bicycle Thieves....................25

Chapter 6   Big Only Counts on the Inside...........31

Chapter 7   Can't Run...Throw a Rock...................37

Chapter 8   Curbside Creekwater.........................43

Chapter 9   Pokeberry Paradise............................49

Chapter 10   Tree Surfing..55

Reviews

"*Dirt Road Doctorate* is not only sincere and full of laughs in the accounts shared, it is powerfully candid and raw.

To anyone that has ever doubted themselves and their abilities because of their past, where they came from, or what they've been through - may Gary's words, recollections, and lessons act as a beacon on your personal dirt road to who you are meant to be - YOU - in all your perfectly-imperfect glory. As the man himself says, "People will follow someone who is going somewhere, even if that somewhere is their own destruction." People are watching you; and at best, you are watching you.

My hope for you, dear reader, is to look back to your past and use it as your greatest asset in your unique marketplace. That is your tactical advantage. With that in mind; wherever you go, find your target, remember to check the vine, master your marketplace, and climb.

It's not often that one has the privilege, and honor, of digging deep into the intimate mind of a Master. May this book remind you of who you are, and where you, and your endeavors, are going."

Coach Nachi

"Looking for the compass to direct you down the right path? Congratulations, this book will take you down a long dirt road full of adventure. You will laugh, you will cry, and you will learn great lessons. Gary Norris takes you on an amazing experience as he folds some of the most impactful moments of his life into lifelong learned business principles. Whether you are a new business owner or a seasoned entrepreneur there is something of value in this book for everyone. Upon completion you will have key fundamental principles and values that will save you years of frustration and aggravation in your future endeavors."

Sean Wyman
Movement Innovator and Author of *Let Go: The Movement Process*

"Dirt Road Doctorate by Gary Gale Norris, from the School of Busted Knuckles is a great book full of insights and stories that bring you back to a childhood of adventures. Get ready for some changes, be prepared—when you expose yourself to the influence of this Busted Knuckle philosophy—to experience a changed life, which may help you not only to negotiate your way through life with harmony and understanding, but also to prepare you for the accumulation of material riches in abundance.

This gem of a book is brimming with insights and profound visionary message. Gary Norris is sure to stimulate, challenge and inspire you. Welcome to a great adventure, welcome to the rest of your life.

You know you've read a good book when you turn the last page and feel a little as if you are saying goodbye to a friend. This is one of those books."

Dr. Chevy Chevere

FOREWARD

Gary Norris is a consultant to millionaires, to bankers, to hospital administrators, and doctors. I highly recommend this book. It will inspire you, and give you practical leadership skills. No matter what business you're trying to turn around or take to the next level. Gary astounds me with his business savvy and intuitive advice. Coming from a dirt road myself. I can relate to the memories and the lessons that a dusty road can bring. I nicknamed Gary the millionaire consultant (MC) after hearing of the many businesses he and his team have turned around. Walk with Gary as he teaches you the world through his eyes. In this book you will find humor in every lesson with a down-home delivery. This book will teach you Business strategy and brilliance. It will give you nuggets to master your market place. It will Inspire you to understand your clients needs, grow as a person, and keep a competitive edge. This book supplies encouragement for those in the business trenches who want to break out of their restraining boundaries. You will Learn to discern between genuine and counterfeit business alliances. And finally for those who have fallen, you will find the courage to climb again.

Pastor Scott Nowlin

PREFACE

I can still feel the cold mountain water around my ankles, climbing up my britches to chill my knees. I can still see the layers of dust on anything that wasn't in motion in the summer. I can still hear each car's unique sound as it left the paved surface of the road at the bottom of the hollar onto our dirt road. It was our dirt road. There have beens seasons when I wasn't readily owning of that special place; the place of my birth. I have come home. The seasons of life have found me trekking up that same dirt road to the place where my outlook on life, business, success, my fellow man, and how to leave a legacy all began. I have peeled back the veil and allowed you, dear reader, into my world. It is sacred to me. While on long business trips, the memories of this place will bring me to deep laughter and even tears. It is my hope and prayer that these stories of my life on this "one lane dirt road' will inspire you, guide you, bring you joy, maybe even tears...but most of all...will deeply impact your view of business and how common sense is not given in college...you are gifted with it by your Creator... and Common Sense, above all degrees and doctorates, is your most valuable asset.

Chapter 1

CAP GUNS AND GAS TANKS
KNOW WHERE TO USE YOUR POWER

The year was 1979. I was a 9-year-old little blond-headed kid with a Southern drawl and bright hazel eyes. My little brother, Gerry, and I loved cap guns. We had learned that the brand of caps would make different "bangs". Some larger and some smaller. The larger ones were more fun and had a larger spark at night. We would wait until almost dark to begin firing our pistols and playing cops and robbers. The best caps would light up at night and make the loudest pop. So much fun.

My dad had a 1953 Dodge truck. Very cool looking. I have no idea what possessed me to do the following, but a great lesson resulted.

This particular truck had a "gooseneck" gas cap. In other words, there was a pipe protruding from the bed with a typical twist on gas cap. I said to my brother, "I bet if I fire this cap gun with these awesome caps in that gooseneck, it would sound amazing!" He readily agreed. So, with him hiding in the bushes nearby, I unscrewed the cap, stuck my little hand and my cap gun down into the gooseneck and...pulled the trigger. The cap gun fired off with a loud bang. It echoed because of the deep tank below. We giggled as two mischievous boys rightly should. So, we decided to do it again. Only this time, I would stick my whole arm down into the gooseneck and see if I could manage to get a greater echo.

What happened next will go down in Norris history. My brother had returned to the safety of the bushes. I submerged my arm with cap gun into the gooseneck and pulled the trigger. Yes, the echo was amazing. Yet... following the echo came a strange rumble. Louder and louder. Then—with panic setting in—I quickly pulled my arm out just in time to see a literal pillar of fire burst from the gooseneck! It was the coolest thing we had ever seen! It lit up the front yard like Christmas...so bright. And the BOOM was earth-shaking!

Upon hearing the loud noise and seeing the front of the house light up, our dad came to the front door and said, "Boys...what are you doing?"

To which I replied from the bushes (next to my half-trembling, half-laughing little brother), "Playing with our cap guns, Dad". Accepting that answer, he quietly went back in the house. My brother and I nearly collapsed from the rush of adrenaline and panic. If we had blown dad's truck up that day...well...I probably wouldn't be writing this. Just saying. I have revisited that story with my family many times. Each time with more laughter than before.

Over the years, I have been both powerless in business and I have had ultimate power. I have been the recipient of abused power and the recipient of power well-placed. It is truly a skill that in this day and time, is polluted, diluted, abused, and misunderstood. Here are the valuable lessons in leadership that your local professor won't share.

1. Authority, leadership, and power is not only a license to rule, but also a license to restore. I have had many opportunities over the last 27 years to do both. I find more joy in restoration than ruling.

2. Leadership is not leadership if no one follows you. People will follow someone who is going somewhere, even if that somewhere is their own destruction. Make sure where you are going is where you want others to end up, because people are following you right now... whether you accept it or not. It may be your children as they want to emulate you, your neighbors as they try to compete with you, your co-workers as they try to collaborate with you, or your employees as they try to accommodate you. Someone, somewhere is following you.

3. Leadership means that when I reach the finish line, I am surrounded by those whom I have taken with me to the finish line. These are the ones I am honored to share the victory with. We have held each other up. We have encouraged each other during the down times. We have given drink to each other when we were thirsty. We have stayed with one another through the minor and major setbacks. We have celebrated each victory.

4. As a leader with power, you have the honor and opportunity to use your power to EMpower others. You also have the opportunity to leave a wake of destroyed lives, hopes, and dreams behind you as you continue your ascent to the lonely top. As business leaders, I urge you right now...make the decision to wield your power for good.

There is a universal law. I know it as sowing and reaping. You may call it karma. Either way, if you are sowing seeds of servanthood with your power, you will reap a bountiful harvest of successful people and businesses all around you. This law applies to every area of life. It is universal and immutable.

5. Know where to use your power. Every person reading this has a unique power. How you use it is up to you. You may light up the night with your power illuminating the way for those following you. You may only hear an echo of what could have been if your power had been well placed and used.

Just today, in the middle of writing this chapter, a business owner reached out to me using social media asking how to be "rich" like me. I smiled. The line of questioning tells me where this business owner's mind and heart are. I responded, *"Money* doesn't make you rich." Then I was given an opportunity to explain how the effective use of power will EMpower people around you to succeed. This is being rich.

Use your power to help those who are just discovering theirs. If you do....you will never reach a finish line alone.

Chapter 2

CHECK THE VINE
DON'T SWING BEYOND YOUR RESEARCH

It has been said that on our dirt road, you have to look straight up to see the sky. There are large Blue Ridge Mountains on both sides. My pappaw bought approximately 100 acres on both mountain sides and chose to raise his family there. It was said that no man could farm those steep mountain sides. He was not one to listen to the voices. He listened to his head and heart. As a result, I have worked the fields he planted on both mountain sides as did my father and his siblings. Apparently, they can be farmed.

These steep and heavily wooded grades provide very nice vine swings for the brave to ride. Once a vine is found, the first step is to free the vine from the ground in such a way that maximum distance can be reached. The second step is to pull vigorously on the vine to make sure it is securely attached to the tree tops above.

One day as my brother, our two cousins, Josh and Joe, and I were exploring the mountainside above the road, we found the Vine-of-All-Vines. It was about three inches thick and very sturdy. We jerked and pulled on the vine to test its ability to hold us as we swung out over the deep ravine below. All seemed safe.

Now comes the fun part. Who goes first. After several minutes of name-calling and tests of manhood, my little brother was selected to go first. Gerry was not one to mess around. He is *still* this way. He backed way up the bank and ran down at full speed hitting the little logging road and launching himself into the great unknown. He swung out for what seemed to be days; letting out a yell the whole way. When he reached the road where we were eagerly awaiting him, he was lit up with excitement. Now, we all wanted a turn because Gerry had survived.

I got to go next. I followed Gerry's example and backed way up the mountainside. I took off at full speed (and we were *very* fast runners). I hit the logging road and jumped with all my might. The wind was racing past my ears. My breath was gone as it seemed I could see for miles. "This must be how Tarzan feels when he is swinging from tree to tree," I thought. I was fully alive!

If you have ever taken a vine ride, you know that you want the ride to last as long as possible. It did last a long time. And then—when I reached maximum distance—there was a POP and the vine dropped about six inches. I looked back at the road where my brother and cousins were cheering. They did not see the vine give. Then...in an instant...SNAP!

Suddenly, I was falling to the mountainside below. As destiny would have it, I landed right in a pile of firewood that Pappaw had been stacking between two trees. Firewood went everywhere. It felt like every bone in my body was broken. I lay there moaning. Finally, when I could gather my wits about me and focus my hearing, I heard all three of the others up on the logging road...laughing! Yes. Laughing. Just as you probably are right now.

I survived. No broken bones—just a broken ego. As I climbed my way to the logging road, I heard my cousin say "Whew! Boy, I sure am glad *we* didn't take that ride." I took one for the team that day.

In business, we have lost the art of searching out the matter. In scripture, Jesus refers to this as "counting the cost". What happens too often is we become enamored with the "ride" and forget to check the vine. Maybe we tug a little, gaze up into the treetops, even swing a little but we don't really commit to searching out the matter before committing to the ride. When we find out that the vine is snapping...it's too late. There are several lessons I have taken from that experience and hope to pass along to you.

1. Make sure you test the tensile strength of your "vine". This could be client commitment to buy, or prospects in the market. It may be projected future growth. It may be market trends. Whatever you are counting on, whatever you are depending on to make that decision, you *must* check "the vine". It's not always enough to just tug a little. Pull with all your might. Make sure it will hold you, your assets, your people, the people that come with the venture, and have a backup plan in case just at the maximum reach...you feel that familiar "snap". If the vine doesn't seem strong enough to hold you and your future, *don't swing*.

2. Look below. Where will you land? The best rides are very high. What is your exit strategy? When developing the exit strategy, make sure to consider ALL the people standing on the logging road. The strategy must include them.

3. Take it all in. The views from up there were amazing. There were vistas from those vine rides that I would never have experienced unless I had launched out. Take it all in. Enjoy it with the people whose blood sweat and tears paved the way for your ride.

Come back with stories. Tell them what to look for when they ride the vine. Share the experience with those who will never have the courage to take the vine in their hands. Let them live the vine ride through your eyes. Your transparency may very well be the thing that one day, causes them to take the vine ride too.

4. Prepare for your return. The most difficult part of riding a vine is the return. You never know which way you will be facing. Very rarely do you land in the same place you took off from. Make sure you have a team wanting to help you back on your feet.

These may be people who know your secret fear of heights. Or people who just enjoy watching you ride. When you get back, make sure these are trusted core group who will do *more* than laugh if the vine breaks. Make sure they are watching, listening, *and* cheering. They will be the first to make sure you are okay if you fall and the first to celebrate with you when you make it back to the road safely.

Great risk often equals great reward. You can mitigate your risk by being deliberate in checking the vine. Make sure to take in the views while you are out there. They are truly amazing.

Chapter 3

EQUAL OPPORTUNITY QUARTERBACK
EVERYONE GETS A CHANCE TO WIN

Touchdown! Most Americans understand that, at the very least, this is something good. Something you want to achieve. A place you want to reach. As a boy, I had dreams of being an NFL quarterback. My dad would spend hours in our backyard showing me the expert mechanics of Fran Tarkenton. I would read for hours about Dan Fouts, Steve Bartkowski, Doug Williams, Roger

Staubach, and Terry Bradshaw. My little brother was a receiver fanatic. He was my go-to in pickup games. He could outrun most defenders and I could get him the ball. I can't remember *ever* turning down a pickup game of football. It wasn't often but, occasionally a couple boys would wander into our yard and ask to play. One summer day, two strange boys walked into the yard and challenged my brother and I to a pickup game. There were two of them and two of us. My brother and I were tougher than most and *definitely* faster than most. We just knew we could whip these fellas. So we accepted.

This is where the story changes. Suddenly, my hero—the strongest man alive—stepped onto the field. My DAD! He walked up and asked us what was going on. We told him that these guys had challenged us to a football game. He replied "Fine. I will be quarterback for both teams." My heart leaped! How awesome. I had seen him throw. I knew he was a smart quarterback. Besides—he was my dad—*surely* we would get the best passes.

Being the "visiting team" dad insisted that we kick off to them. So, with that, the game was on. It was tight. We were fast. They were fast too. They scored. We scored. Incredible passes were being offered up to both teams. And as the game progressed, I noticed that my jealousy rose. I was angry! How could dad be throwing the same great passes to them as he was to us?

We had set a final score limit. My brother and I had scored. The visiting team had the last reception. The ball was hiked. Dad dropped back and four boys raced down the sidelines. My brother's determination to prevent the winning touchdown was matched only by my own. Running a slant route into our homemade touchdown area, the guy I was covering slipped just in front of me. With the accuracy of Mr. Tarkenton himself, dad released a bullet down the field that was right on the money. My sworn enemy stretched out and caught the pass. "We win!" exclaimed the two boys. And my dad was the reason.

Being the gentleman that my dad is, he made us congratulate the strangers. On the way back to the house my dad made a profound statement. He said "Boys, they won fair and square. I gave both teams 100% and they won. Make sure you beat them next time."

In a moment of anger, I discovered how much I loved my dad. He was truly my hero.

Are you the "full time quarterback"? Are you giving 100% to everyone around you even if your think they are not on your team? My dad is a man of justice and fairness. He showed me that day that everyone has the chance to win. We get the same passes. Sometimes the difference comes down to who has the ball last. In business, I have revisited this story many times. I have had co-workers and employees who seemed to be my enemies. Then, I remembered my dad. He threw the same passes to everyone on the field. This memory encourages me to do the same. The morals of this story for us are these:

1. Challenges are not insults. This may have been our first downfall that day. We took personally the challenge of these boys. Our focus on our own superiority instead of their ability may have blinded us to the opportunity. We lost the opportunity to rise above the challenge and become victorious.

2. There are always *two* end zones. In business, victories come in different shapes and sizes. Touchdowns are achieved by gaining 10 yards at a time. Each person has an opportunity to reach their end zone. It may come in one glorious Hail Mary pass or a series of small victories. There are many people on your team. When your team is counting on you to throw a good pass to them or one of your teammates, will you make sure that you throw a catchable pass?

3. The playing field is *level*. Everyone in your company starts at the same level. They come in the same door you do every day. Their families depend on your ability to throw an accurate pass at the right time. In my companies, we are in this together. Ask any of my teammates and they will tell you that "Gary is one of us. We can talk to him." Value the players on your team. No man is an island.

4. Show up to the game. I had no doubt that my dad would be there for my brother and I. However, I did not expect that he would throw the same passes to our rivals. He came to play full-out for everyone on the field. When the day is over, can you look back on the field and see that you gave 100% for EVERYONE that showed up? Did you reserve something special for the inner circle? Was there a poorly thrown pass to influence the game one way or another?

I urge you. When you go to sleep tonight, your rest will be sweeter if you can close your eyes knowing that you left it all on the field. For those who seemingly deserve your best...and those who may *not*.

I am in no way endorsing the casting of your pearls before swine. Don't waste your energies on those who are self-serving. However, those around you who have the interest of the team at heart. They are counting on you. Be an equal opportunity quarterback. You won't regret it.

In closing, we never saw those guys again. Maybe that is best. The lessons of that game are with me still. And my dad....he is still my hero.

Chapter 4

"NEVER LEARN NO YOUNGER"
ALWAYS BE A STUDENT

My pappaw was a big man. All the men in my family are big. At least...to me. I am 5'6". My pappaw was 6'1". My dad is 6'. My little brother is 6'1". Pappaw was one of my all time heroes. Strong and fearless. A trait that runs in my family. He was always working the land. Cultivating and reaping from its bounty. He was the guy who had ginseng planted in random places around his 100 acres and knew exactly where each tiny plant was located. He would split locust post for fencing and sell it to the community. He would cut firewood from his land and deliver to the widows in winter. He would gather native leaves and berries for drying and sell them to the local compounding pharmacy.

Every day at 5 a.m., he could be found in his chair reading his large print Bible. He was brave and honorable. He wore bib overalls everywhere. Even to church. A pack of Wrigley's or Juicy Fruit could always be found in the bib pocket. While sitting beside him at Sunday school, he would look over quietly at my brother and I. Gently gesturing with his hand, he would slip a piece of gum to us from that famous pocket. He was the kind of man who said what he meant and meant what he said... and everyone in that community and beyond knew this about him.

One day as we were finishing up one of Mammaw's famous endless breakfasts, Pappaw got up from the table and said to my brother and me, "Finish up boys. We got work to do." Excitement gripped us because working with Pappaw was always and adventure and more often than not, it was to be a learning experience.

We followed him to one of his barns where he kept his wood cutting tools. There it was. I could almost hear angels singing. The one...the only....red chainsaw. HALLELUJAH! He picked it up and we headed out into the sunlight almost giddy with anticipation. We walked over to where he had a new pile of unfinished locust posts. These were to be split and trimmed into fence posts for the community to purchase as needed. He stood looking at the pile of logs as if to ask them for a volunteer.

After selecting the first log, we knew the lesson was about to begin. Turning to us like a sage of woodworking wonders, he looked at me and asked me a question I never forgot. He said, "Have you ever run a chainsaw?"

I said, "No sir".

This is what rocked me to my core. He said, "Well, you'll never learn no younger". With that, he choked the chainsaw and after a couple of yanks on the angry machine, I was wrapping my 12-year-old hands around its powerful trigger. That day, though I am sure I did not gain any height, when we sat down for supper, I was certain I had grown several inches and could finally hang out with the grown-ups at Sunday dinner.

In my business experience, I have discovered a famine of learning. Now, let me clarify. I am not referring to book smarts. I am referring to an old-fashioned "I-don't-know-how-to-do-that-right-now-but-give-me-a-little-time-and-I-am-confident-I-can-figure-it-out" attitude. A fearless, insatiable desire to learn. You will hear me say it often. Master YOUR marketplace. It truly is your best and truest advantage. However, many entrepreneurs aren't committed to learning. Perhaps it's for fear of failure or falling short.

That day as I gripped that chainsaw I was terrified *and* fully alive. My pappaw was holding my hands and standing behind me the entire time. I was safe. This is a larger lesson than any of us realize. I hope you get it.

Life is full of learning opportunities. Every moment of every day could hold a unique opportunity to grow.

You may have the opportunity to expand your understanding of client's needs, competitive advantage, market traction, or just a deeper understanding of yourself, your gifts, and talents. What will you do with it? Will you seize the opportunity to expand yourself? Your knowledge? Will you take hold of the tool that is much more powerful than anything you have handled to date? Will you allow the opportunity to stretch your perception of reality and grow you in ways that can only make you stronger, braver, and wiser? The morals of this story for our businesses are these:

1. Embrace that you don't know everything. The sooner you realize that your are still a student, the sooner you will be able to mine every day for its great and beautiful learning experiences. These experiences will set you apart from everyone else in your marketplace and provide you with the advantages you need to win.

2. Seek out the opportunity hidden within every day to learn something new. They are there. Don't fear them. Chase them. Tackle them. Overcome them. Master them. These opportunities will stretch you. They will bend you. They may even frighten you. But in the end, they will sharpen you.

3. Make sure you have a guide. I would have not taken the chainsaw that day had not one of the strongest people I knew been guiding me during the experience. There are people in your circles who will guide your learning experience. Allow them to be there. They will celebrate with you when you realize that you have acquired a new skill.

4. You will never learn 'no younger'. Don't stop being a student. Time is not slowing down. The best teachers in my life are still students. I will be a student for life. I have discovered the joy of learning. I am an insatiable student. Be fearless to pursue a new skill or enter an arena that is new. Always be ready to admit that you have no idea what the answer is BUT...be relentless in pursuit of the answer. My dad has said very often, "When you have learned enough to live, you have lived enough to die."

Never stop learning. It is life. Besides, you never know when someone in your neck of the woods may need a good chainsaw operator.

Chapter 5

BICYCLE THIEVES
KNOW YOUR ALLIES AND
ENEMIES WON'T EXIST.

It was a Schwinn Lemon Peeler Special. My dad's oldest brother had purchased a bike for my brother and me. It was beautiful. My first real bike. It had a spring-loaded banana seat, long forks, and a five-speed to boot. The gear-shift was on the center frame and could be shifted like a muscle car. I *loved* that bike.

One day, my brother and I were riding in our yard when the Anderson brothers walked up. I must describe the Anderson boys. They were the consummate bullies. The older of the two was in high school and the youngest was in my class. They were...well...they were just downright mean. They had a reputation for double-teaming in fights and fighting dirty. They were feared as heartless outlaws. When my brother and I realized they had entered our safe world, I can still feel the panic and terror in my gut. Would they murder us and bury us behind the barn? Could we get away and safely into the house before they pummelled us like dirty rugs? Unlikely.

What happened next was a boy's worst nightmare. The oldest Anderson walked up and said, "Hey...give us those bikes!" We resisted but to no avail. Violently and forcefully, they took our bikes and disappeared over the hill towards our elementary school.

Broken and downtrodden, defeated and hopeless, we sat down on the front porch steps. I can't remember the thoughts that controlled my young mind but I can remember that my brother and I sat and wept together. I love my brother. He is my blood. We are only 14 months apart. Very close. He too is one of my heroes. I can still see the rage in his eyes. The rage that mirrored what I was feeling inside.

After what seemed like an eternity void of light and hope, the familiar sound of my dad arriving home from work broke the silence. A hard-working father with a metal lunch box and ball cap strolled up the walk toward his broken-hearted boys. I can see the look on his face as if it were this morning. "Boys," he said, "Whats wrong?"

"The Anderson boys stole our bikes," I quickly replied, slipping into uncontrollable tears.

Very calmly and quietly, he placed his lunchbox on the porch, he said "Which way did they go?". Unable to speak, my brother and I pointed in unison towards the school. He looked at us both and said, "I will be right back".

Now. Let me interject here. My dad is a man's man. He is no joke. Every person that ever met him knew he was the real deal. Fearless and brave. A man of God. A man of justice. When dad said, "I will be right back", he meant *with* our bikes! He walked up the road toward the school. We didn't go with him, but we didn't need to.

In just a few minutes, my brother and I could see Dad coming over the hill with our bikes...*and* the Anderson boys were STILL attached! Yes! They were still in the seats! Now *they* were crying. Dad had each one by the back of their necks and was leading them very quickly towards our house. He rolled them into our yard and up to the front porch. Tightening his grip on their necks, he said, "Now, apologize to my boys!" Through painful tears, they humbly apologized and returned our bikes.

As they were leaving, Dad ensured they would never return with sternly stating to them, "NEVER come into my yard again and stay away from my boys...or you will deal with ME! Do you understand?"

They sheepishly replied, "Yes sir."

"Now go!" Dad ordered. They wisely obliged. I'm not sure what we enjoyed more...having our bikes back or seeing the Anderson boys defeated. Either way, that was an epic day of victory for my little brother and me.

Business is often like that. You are riding your bike in your safe place, and suddenly out of nowhere, something goes wrong. Your competition steals a client, or moves in next door, or cuts the tires on your bike. Maybe they steal the bike itself and tout it to the marketplace as their own. Feeling helpless, you believe all you can do is watch. Here is what I learned that dreadful and wonderful day:

1. Knowing my enemy didn't equip me for defending my property. We knew the enemy. We were aware of the stories. We had witnessed the carnage. When it came our turn, there was nothing we could do. I am convinced that mastering your marketplace is more about knowing *yourself* than the competition. Yes, you must know them and their services or products in order to provide something superior. But the most important knowledge is the knowledge of YOU. Know who you are. You are the imperative. You are the watershed moment. You are economic stimulus. Know you. There is only ONE of you and you are fearfully and wonderfully made. Know you.

I was my dad's son. That was credential enough to have calmed my broken heart...but in the distress, I had forgotten my next point.

2. Knowing your allies is pivotal. That day, knowing my enemy did not return our bikes. If knowing our enemy was all we had, we would have never ridden those bikes again. The power of the moment came when our ally arrived. I had forgotten who my greatest ally was...Dad. If I had remembered this, I would have calmly sat down with my brother on the porch and *waited* for certain salvation. But I had forgotten who my ally was. Knowing who your competition is important but also can be distracting. Knowing who your ALLIES are is crucial. It will dictate how you meet each competitor.

3. Your *enemies* don't know who your allies are. The Anderson boys didn't know who my dad was. They would soon learn that when my brother and I were powerless to save ourselves, there was an ally who would stop at nothing to restore that which was taken away. Are you thinking of that person in your company who has fought for you when no one was looking? Who went to bat for you when there was nothing in it for them? How about that team of leaders who show up day in day out to make sure your product or service makes it to the marketplace intact and that your business is the standard of excellence. What your competition doesn't know is who your allies are.

What they don't have is YOUR TEAM. That is your unstoppable advantage. Dad didn't say anything to us when the Anderson boys left. He didn't have to. His actions said all we needed to hear. He loved his boys..and there was nothing he wouldn't do for us. That is all we needed to know. And we never forgot it.

Chapter 6

BIG ONLY COUNTS ON THE INSIDE
STRENGTH FROM STRUGGLES

485 miles. That is an insurmountable distance when you are alone. I was living in Dover, Delaware. I had just gone through what—at that time—was the most crushing experience. I had lost everything. I had found a kind lady who was willing to rent a small room in her two-bedroom apartment out to a complete stranger. I had a black trash bag of clothes and a box of personal memories. I slept on the floor with my bag of clothes as a pillow.

My mammaw found out that I didn't even have blankets. So, she began making quilts and mailing them to me. On each quilt she would write notes in marker to encourage me and say that she loved me. She would mail me letters that were very long and would barely fit in an envelope. Oh, how I loved her handwriting. Many times I would melt into the corner of that room reading about the weather back on the dirt road. She would update me on how my family was faring. She would share Bible verses with me. She always ended her letters with, "Stay close to Jesus and I will too."

I finally found someone giving away a cot. I gladly took it. It was a folding metal frame model. To me, it was heaven. I was working in an auto detail shop in downtown Wilmington. Some friends found out that I didn't have a car, so they gave me a 1982 Buick LeSabre. What a car! It had a metal coat hanger for an antenna and a masking tape roll for a cup holder. I loved that car.

During one of our phone conversations, my mom and dad had offered to pay for my gas back to Delaware if I could get to that dirt road. I agreed. So, I saved up as much as I could and, after getting the green light to take off work for a week, I took off for home. It was September. I made it to our homeplace and, oh, how wonderful it was to be with people who loved me no matter what. I had been stripped of dignity. Crushed. I wasn't even sure of who I was anymore. Dad and Mom had planned the week knowing I need to be with loved ones so as aunts and uncles, cousins and friends, and grandparents administered the healing power of family and unconditional love, I began to feel human again.

Dad had a 1973 Harley Davidson he was restoring as

a project. He always had a muscle car or something that someone had abandoned. He could see the potential. He could see beyond the dent and cracks. He saw past the fault and saw the need. One day during that blissful week, Dad and I were working on his Harley. We were engrossed in the work. Without skipping a beat, my dad said something to me I never forgot. I will never get over it.

In my moment of lowest self esteem, of brokenness and hurt, he reached me. He said, "Son, you may be small on the outside but to me, you are a big man on the inside. Don't you ever forget that." At that moment, I could have leaped a tall building in a single bound. My hero, the strongest man I have ever known, just reached way past all the dents and scratches and with one statement pushed back the pain I was experiencing. He saw past my faults and ministered to my need. It was a simple statement, but that day changed my life. It set me on a different course.

In business, we often forget that the people who make up our teams, our companies, our departments, are just that...people. They are broken, hurting, flawed, and often times, left to rust in the junkyard. They have been viewed by society as having too many miles or too many dents; a total loss. In fact, they may have even given up on themselves. I had.

Then one day, someone sees the potential. The glint of original paint. The sparkle of chrome. Someone believes in them. Realizing that the struggles that caused those dents and scars are what makes us strong. Makes us resilient. Makes us unstoppable. Those dents prove we are not talking from sideline commentary but from frontline experience. We have something valuable to bring to the table, boardroom, and business. We are big on the inside. When you look at your people, when you have your Monday morning meetings, I pray you see the people in that room completely different. I hope you will consider the following truths:

1. Your words have the power of life *and* death. You don't know what the receptionist has gone through in the last few days. You don't go home with that sales rep. You have no idea where the custodian lays his head at night. There are so many voices today that speak death. They portray a life that most of us will never realize. They can paint a picture of happiness that is shallow and fleeting. There are voices that scream "you are worthless" or "you are too dented" or "you will never get past the place where you are now". STOP! Speak LIFE! The words you say to that broken soul may be the very ones that help them to their feet and allow them to take another step.

2. People are more than their earning potential. People are flesh and blood with hunger and thirst. They enjoy embraces. They crave laughter. They like hot coffee on a cold morning. They are you and me.

So often in my life, I have been defined by what I can deposit in the bank. There is much more to me than my earnings. There is much more to you. There is much more to them. Treat them as the very precious creation that they are. Beautiful in every way. Let their pain become perfume. Let their scars become strength. Let their hurts become honesty. Let their dents become their diamonds.

3. Big only counts on the inside. Our titles mean nothing. Our check stubs are worthless. Our corner offices and expensive cars mean nothing if we cannot reach others and be reached by others. If we are untouchable, then we are *unusable*. Be BIG. Choose to be bigger than every voice that is telling them they are worthless. Choose to be bigger than every sideways look or comment. Choose to be like my dad...and remember that big only counts on the inside.

They need to hear it...but maybe more importantly, you need to say it. The healing accomplished by those words...may be your own.

Chapter 7

CAN'T RUN...THROW A ROCK
BEING EFFECTIVE BEYOND BOUNDARIES

Growing up on a dirt road creates a unique experience when it comes to having kids to hang out with. Namely... there aren't many. Most of us on that road had chores and worked during our free time. Dad and Mom always had a large garden and when we weren't in school we were hoeing something or picking beans or corn. I can remember friends riding their dirt bikes across the mountain to see if my brother and I could play, only to find that we were working. It was good for us and has translated into my ability to typically outwork most people. But when we did have free time, it was rowdy! We had a blast. Sling shots, BB guns, creek swimming, and tree climbing. Fist fighting, knife swapping, and snake hunting. Our closest neighbor was a dairy farmer. His youngest son was our age so we had become close. We did everything together: my little brother, Tommy, and me. The three amigos. We fought hard and played hard. It was the code of dirt road friends.

As a rule, we could not ride our bikes past our mailbox on one end of the road and a specific light pole on the other end of our road. The span was approximately a half mile. One day while my brother was playing with his truck in the dirt at the end of our driveway, I saw Tommy running up the road. I was perched on the front steps with a very good view of what was about to happen. Tommy—at full gallop—ran past our mailbox, into our driveway, and with all his might, hit my brother in the side of his head. He then quickly ran just past the mailbox line where he know we couldn't go. I sprinted from the steps to where my brother was crying. Finding him with nothing more than a bruised ego, I looked up with all the anger and rage an eleven-year-old could muster. I ran up to our "line" where Tommy was doing the "nah nah na nah nah" dance.

I refused to break the rules. I began to beg him to come back across the line. He refused. He knew that I would have beat him down. So, realizing how furious I was, he took off running. Thinking quick on my feet, I grabbed the largest rock I could find, and took aim. He was running at a dead sprint towards his house. Time was not on my side. With the precision of an experienced kid twice my age, I launched the rock into the air hoping it would find its resting place right on his head. In what seems to me now as slow motion, the rock came down with a loud thud...squarely on Tommy's head! Immediately, he crumpled to the dirt road surface with a shriek.

After unleashing a string of violent threats and ultimatums, and with a victory dance that only an eleven-year-old boy could perform, I turned my attentions to my brother. We went into our house and mom began to dress his ego and clean his tear-stained cheeks. Before long, dad announced that we were going to the grocery store. This meant *all* of us. So, we piled into the car and down the road we went. With anger still burning a hole in my gut, we approached Tommy's house. As we drove by, my brother and I both looking toward the house. We saw Tommy. He was sitting under a tree in his front yard, holding a beach towel, soaked with blood. I looked at my brother with my mouth wide open. Silently, we knew we had taught Tommy a lesson.

When we returned home, we noticed that Tommy was not under the tree. Assuming he had stopped the bleeding, we went about our day. But before long, I saw Tommy coming up the road toward our house, blood soaked towel in hand, crying. He quietly walked past us onto our porch and politely knocked at the door. Seeing all the blood my mom said, "Tommy...What happened?" He looked at me with fear rising in his eyes.

Through the pain he sobbed, "Gary hit me in the head with a rock". Without hesitation, my mom glared at me with parental disdain. Leaping to defend myself, I told her the whole story. After pleading with Tommy to tell his dad about the injury, who was working in a pasture nearby, Mom informed Tommy that he needed stitches, and, according to my mom, I needed a spanking.

After my brother's assailant had left, my mom looked at me and said, "I'll be right back". Returning with our family paddle, I expected the worst. Here comes another pivotal moment. With love and compassion my mom looked at me and said, "I am very proud of you for defending your brother. Next time, try to use something other than a rock". With that, I grew ten feet in ten seconds. I bent over and like a man with honor and I took my medicine.

Many times in my professional career, I have had to master the art of operating outside my boundaries. Most business owners and entrepreneurs operate within their familiar boundaries. These are comfort zones. Safe zones of familiarity and complacency. Places where there are no challenges or obstacles. Places where things rarely happen that challenge the status quo or "the way it's always been". I have learned over the years how to leave my comfort zone and thrive. This involves cultivating a demeanor of assimilation that is blindingly quick. I have often said if I don't know the answer today, give me eight hours and I will find it. God has blessed me this way. I learn fast. If you are a business owner or aspiring entrepreneur, let me share a few things with you that might help you when standing at the boundary, contemplating the next step, whether it will be forward into the great unknown or backward into your familiar safe places.

1. Don't step just to be stepping...Step with *purpose*. Launch out deliberately. Leap intentionally. There are others watching, wondering what you will do. You are setting the standard for someone. The only thing to fear out there is the fear itself. I have proved that when I stepped into that place, I found everything I needed to thrive and succeed. The tools are there. Step with purpose.

2. You will fall down. Guaranteed...and it's okay. We all fall down. Winners get back up and step again. Keep stepping and before you know it, you have reached the next level.

3. Have a target. Some will tell you to leave your comfort zone just to be doing it. I disagree. For me, the value comes in knowing my target. It could be a learning experience or acquiring a new skill. It may even be a new journey of growth or fulfillment. Have a target. See it clearly. Determine to overtake it...and you will. Tommy thought his legs could carry him beyond my reach. He didn't consider that I could operate with great effectiveness beyond my boundary. He learned different. Let the marketplace know in no uncertain terms that you are comfortable operating outside your comfort zone... and you can do so with efficiency and effectiveness.

Assimilate quickly. Learn fast. What you will discover is that the boundaries begin to disappear. And take my mom's advice...use something other than a rock.

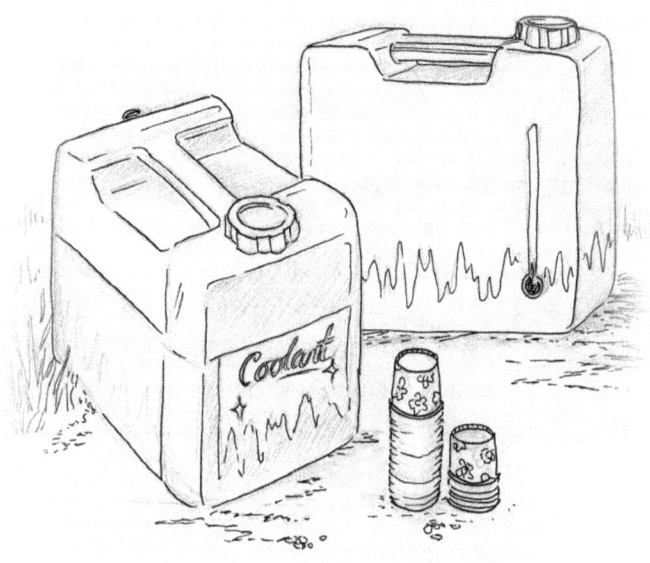

Chapter 8

CURBSIDE CREEKWATER
THE POWER OF DETERMINATION

I don't remember if the summer of 1975 was particularly hot. I am sure it was hot somewhere. What I do remember, is learning a valuable business lesson that day. It was a typical summer day for my brother and me. Getting up...having breakfast...wondering what we were going to do. I am not sure where I got the idea but I am almost positive it came from a TV show or commercial. For whatever reason, my brother and I decided to set up a roadside stand...to sell water. There was a mountain branch that ran from the ridge all the way to a much larger creek at the bottom of our hollar. It was always singing and ice cold. When nothing else could be heard, it's song filled the night.

Let me pause to say something here about that branch. Over the years I have come to love the sound of flowing water. Not the silent deep slow moving rivers, but the glorious sound of whitewater and mountain rivers. What I have come to learn about life from these creeks and branches is that it is the stones beneath give the river its voice. Placed there by God in ages past, their rough surfaces become smooth as the water flows over them. When the Creator wants to create a symphony of sound, He sends a great rain or thaw and fills the creek banks. When He desires a softer sonnet, He holds back the water and enjoys its whisper. Men will try to silence the creek by dredging or damming it in an effort to harness it power or resources. When they are successful, the creek becomes silent.

People are a lot like creeks. They spend inordinate amounts of time trying to remove the stones placed in their lives by the Creator, when it's these very stones that make our lives a beautiful song. Dancing, twisting, turning, rippling. Without the stones beneath, our lives would be silent. The challenges, struggles, hurdles, and obstacles are what make our lives a song. Embrace the twists and turns. These are the notes of your lifesong.

Back to the story. After consulting my business partner (my little brother), we decided that today we would set up a water stand at the end of our driveway by the road. Surely someone would come by and need a drink. We would capitalize on the great demand. The reality is we probably on had a total of five or six cars pass in a day. It was a one lane road...certainly not a busy expressway.

We set out to find the materials. We secured Dixie cups from my mom to provide to weary travellers. Now... what to keep the water in? Aha! Behind my dad's workshop we found two empty antifreeze containers. Great! Now for the water. We made our way to the branch and filled up the antifreeze containers. I know. At this point, you are probably saying, "*Gross*, water in antifreeze containers? Who will buy that?" I fully agree. But I was six. I hadn't learned the skill of thinking things through completely at that age.

With our cups, creek water filled containers, and determination we promptly set up our first business by the road....and waited. Eventually our first customer came slowing driving up the road. Seeing two little boys standing by the road with antifreeze containers, he stopped. I don't remember who he was. I do remember he was a buyer. When he had stopped his car next to us, he got out and engaged us in business. "What are you fellas doing?"

Then I eagerly explained our business model. "Selling water."

"How much?" he asked.

I replied, "A nickel a cup."

He wasted no time and said, "Well, I will take two." With that he handed my brother and me each a nickel. I couldn't believe it. *This was working!* Soon, another car came by and...*the same result!* We were going to be rich! We had each earned a dime and our overhead was $0 (a business model I have tried to replicate with limited success). It wasn't long before our mail man came driving up the road. He had to stop anyway to deliver the mail. When he came to a stop and had placed our mail in the box, he began conversation. "Fellas, what do you have there?"

I had my pitch down. "We are selling water."

"Tell me, are those antifreeze jugs?" He dug a little deeper.

"Yes sir," I replied.

"Where did you get the water?" he asked.

"From the creek," I quickly responded, certain he would appreciate our thoughtfulness in providing cold creek water to weary travellers.

"And how much are you selling that water for?" he asked.

"A nickel a cup." I had this sales thing down.

"I will make you an offer," he said. We lit up. "I will give you each a dollar if you will make me a promise. Give me all the water and never sell water by the road again. Do we have a deal?"

A dollar? Each?! We had made it to the big time in one day! "YES SIR!"

He found two one-dollar bills in his pocket, gave them to us, and we gave him the containers. A new business launch and acquisition in one day! Now that's getting it done!

It never ceases to amaze me the different kinds of people who are set up by the road hoping someone will come by, either by accident or obligation, who will be in need of their products and services. We are—as a general rule of thumb — pretty passive. We think that just because we hang out a shingle and open for business, people will be clamoring to do business with us. If this is a reality for you, I am thrilled. For most of us, every day is a new battle. There are several lessons in this story. I pray they become clear for you now.

1. Be creative in sourcing. I see this every day in my consulting. If you will dig a little deeper, you can often find lower costs and better quality. And many times they are closer to you than you think. Stay local if possible. We have forgotten the power that local economy plays in the success of our own businesses. I work with entrepreneurs worldwide. I consult with incubators that are raising up the next generation of Steve Jobs and Warren Buffets. However, I know my first marketplace is in my town. When they succeed, I succeed. My roots are here. Not in South Africa, or Europe, or Asia. I often quote Psalms 1, "He will be like a tree, planted by rivers of water." I am a tree planted in this local community of businesses and the river of water (or creek in my case) is close by. Be committed to your local resources and ensure they are successful first. This will have insurmountable impact on your business as well. Source locally.

2. Tap into sustainable resources. There was no worry that we would have an endless supply of water. I don't ever remember the creek drying up. It is as strong today as it was when my dad was growing up on the same road. Find resources that are naturally sustainable. These often come with the lowest cost and highest quality.

3. Corner your market. We knew there wouldn't be many travellers. *But,* we also knew they couldn't ignore us. We had our market cornered. They had no choice but to stop and inquire as to what these cute little boys were doing standing by the road holding antifreeze jugs. They had to acknowledge us. In your marketplace, be un-ignorable. Be unforgettable.

4. Stand on the roads everyone else overlooks. Find a marketplace that people have overlooked. There are customers in that place. There are clients in that place. They have needs and wants too. Find them. You will discover that their money spends and deposits just like the big city money does.

5. Listen to every offer. That doesn't mean you have to accept it. But always listen. One thing I have learned to do well and have come to really enjoy is listening. Listen. Be patient to respond but first always listen. The offers may be terrible. The ideas may be unfeasible. The goals may be unrealistic. But you will never know if you don't listen. We are too often dismissive of people's ideas or their input. Listen. Engage the conversation.

Don't be afraid of the conversation. You may learn something and get a dollar or two in the process.

Chapter 9

POKEBERRY PARADISE
KNOW THE DIFFERENCE BETWEEN GOOD FRUIT AND POISON FRUIT

The end of our driveway seemed to us like a gateway to the rest of the world... another dimension. Even though it only led to another dirt road, there were endless possibilities out there. If you were out with us playing on any given summer day, you would notice the large and seemingly vivacious plants. They were very colorful and, at the right time of year, hanging absolutely full of berries. These berries are purple and hang in clusters just like grapes. To a five-year-old and six-year-old, they look mighty tempting.

One day as my brother and I were playing at the Gateway to the Great Unknown, we decided to fill our bellies with the bounty of those glorious plants. To us, we were eating grapes. After the glorious buffet of pokeberries had been consumed and the plants stripped bare, we went in to announce to our mom that we had discovered and consumed bushels of grapes. Now, pokeberries *will* stain. They were used by Native Americans as a dye. So, upon seeing the purple stain on our faces and clothes, she very wisely demanded, "Show me where you found the 'grapes'". We proceeded to the end of our driveway where we had been dining and the look of horror was unmistakable.

The next thing I remember is being whisked away to the emergency room at our local hospital. I remember the nurse saying, "Drink this," and handing me a cup of water. The first 3 or 4 cups were pretty good. From the 5th cup on...I started to not feel so great. Then... well...you can fill in the blank as to what happened next. It was the old fashioned version of "pumping the stomach". I never forgot *that* lesson. They may look like beautiful grapes...but what they really are, is poisonous and deadly.

So many times in my business life, I have seen what looked like the ideal client, ideal sale, or perfect business alliance. I have taken the fruit and found that in the end, I had to have my proverbial stomach pumped. What I was *so* convinced to be exactly what I needed ended up to be the very thing or person who would end up becoming my undoing without a trip to the emergency room or reality. I can see some of you saying, "Yep... that's me," nodding your head in agreement. We fix our gaze upon the glistening fruit and before we know it we feel the familiar hunger pains. In a flash, we begin shoveling that stuff in like there is no tomorrow. So, before your cheeks and clothes turn purple (which will never wash out, by the way), let me suggest that you consider a few things *I* learned that day.

1. Not everything that looks like a grape...is a grape. The only way I could have known that the pokeberries were not grapes, was to be intimately acquainted with grapes. Let me say it another way. To save yourself the trip to the emergency room, become intimately acquainted with the *right* thing and the *wrong* thing will look pathetic. My knowledge of the right thing was deficient, therefore I could not identify the wrong thing as just that—wrong. Acquaint yourself intimately with excellence, with healthy and good things, and things that are subpar, or bad for you, or even *questionable* will become repulsive.

2. Embrace the order of learning. Sometimes we will learn a valuable lesson by experiencing what we shouldn't do. This comes from getting into the fire and realizing you will now bear the scars of that experience. Other times, we learn by simply investigating the matter out. I mentioned the concept of "checking the vines" earlier. Do the homework. It's okay to say, "I just don't know enough yet. I will have to wait to make a decision about that until my homework has been done". I have come to love this position. Don't swing out until you know the vine is securely attached. This is no guarantee that you will not fall or get poisoned. However, it will mitigate your risk significantly.

Sometimes we can learn by watching others eat the berries and get sick. Almost like the "Mikey" commercials from years ago. The boys around the table are discussing who will try the cereal first. Mikey does and likes it, so it must be safe for the rest of them. This type of learning is available but rarely used. We see people get hurt. We see businesses close. We watch relationships crumble. Yet, we do not salvage the lessons available to us for our own good.

3. Become intimately acquainted with RIGHT.
We are a stubborn bunch. It's true. Once, I was described by a dear friend as the guy who runs across the minefield losing limbs along the way. When I reach the other side, instead of announcing, "Whew...I won't do that again!", I confidently reply, "Okay...now that I know where all the mines are...LET'S DO THIS AGAIN!".

What is in us that causes us to run straight back to the end of the driveway and start shoveling in pokeberries knowing that in just a few hours we will be right back at the emergency room drinking more water than we ever wanted? Maybe it's the resilient human spirit. Maybe it's hard-headed resolve. Maybe it's stupidity. Regardless of what it is, it is. Learning is a gift. Some of us are quick learners. Some of us *never* learn. Some of us are a mixture of both.

It all starts at doing your homework. Study methods are different for everyone but we *all* get homework. You have to do the homework and take the test before you get the grades. No one ever gets the grade before the homework and test. Try to minimize losses. When you do suffer losses, learn everything you can. Don't go back the way you came. The only way to know a counterfeit is to be such an expert with the real thing that even the most minute deviation is like a screaming billboard. I strive to be intimately acquainted with what is right so that when wrong skips into my path, it would be insanity to partake.

To this day, when I see pokeberries, I go back to that magical driveway where anything was possible, any destination reachable, and I could become anything...except immune to pokeberry paradise.

Chapter 10

TREE SURFING
THE BEST VIEW COMES AFTER THE CLIMB

Mountain vistas are unforgettable. I will never get over them. I am convinced God smiles a lot. If those breathtaking scenes are His vantage point every day... He certainly smiles a ton. Me, I get up there and catch my breath, worship my Creator, weep at His vast power, and marvel that He thinks of me. He loves me. He loves you. As a child, those views were my drug. For my brother as well. We would work half the day to get to a place where we could see for miles. We accomplished this by what we call 'tree surfing'. Here is how it works. From the ground, find what looks to be the highest tree around. Then, start your ascent. Climb very carefully to ensure safe arrival to the very top of the tree. If the tree is strong enough, it will support you to the very top. Once you reach the top, you find a safe and sturdy branch to sit on and then, the magic happens. You poke your head just above the canopy of trees and the rest is history.

Most people aren't aware that there is a different kind of breeze up there. It is a strong breeze with a voice. It speaks. I can hear it now. It brings tears. It brings laughter. It brings joy. Those views are reserved for the brave. The fearless. For those who dare to climb to the very top and take it all in.

We spent hours up there. The surfing aspect is that the trunk of the tree is very nimble at that height so when the winds blow, your extra weight will cause the tree to sway. Pretty dangerous, I suppose. However, the joy of being up there far outweighed the danger to us. I can still hear the sounds. Whoever breached the canopy first would yell to the other one, "Where are you? You *gotta* see this!" Eventually all parties would be peeking out of the tops of those venerable and patient trees. Hours we would stay up there. I can hear the wind singing songs of peace now. It was cool and filled with perfume of a million flowers. Pappaw's bee hives could be seen from up there. Occasionally I could see my uncle walking around his yard or weeding his garden. We could hear the creek below, calling to us, cheering us on. I would look out over those rolling mountains and think, "One day I'm going to come back and visit with you for a while. I want you to tell me all the stories you know." The mountains talked back in their own way.

We would stay up there until we heard the familiar "Boys! Time for supper". With great disdain—and only because we were very hungry—we would dismount the great timber holding us high enough to see what we thought was the whole world. It would take some time to get down but we eventually were back on the ground and sprinting down the familiar paths that led us home. "Where have you boys been?" Mom would ask.

"Climbing trees again," we would reply and then attempted to describe beauty the best way little boys know how. I intend to surf trees again. When I do, it will be as powerful an experience as ever it was.

Our business culture is one of quick success and fast money. I see it all the time on social media. People posting pictures of expensive stuff: watches, cars, houses... stuff. At least three times per day, someone invites me to connect with them so they can show me how to work less and gain more freedom. But, I don't hear anything about the *climb*. I don't hear anything about the change in other people's lives. I hear a lot about improving *my* life, but not the lives of other people. They don't know me. They have no idea what is valuable to me. They have no idea the busted knuckles and sore backs it took to get me where I am today. They disregard the careful selection of limbs to ascend to the top. Listen...success isn't stuff. Believing that lie is like winning a triathlon and when the judge hands you the trophy, you respond with, "No thank you. I just want the cheap plastic tape I crossed at the finish line". Setting your sites on "stuff" instead of the real prize is the pinnacle of futility. When you reach the finish line, I pray that there are so many people crossing with you that you cross the line on their shoulders. Show people how to reach the top. Don't tell them. Take them with you. Those moments gazing out from the canopy taught me some valuable lessons.

1. You have to leave the stable earth to get there. A conscious decision is made. A pivotal moment is seized. A difficult word spoken. An embrace. Forgiveness. Faith. Hope. Love. All very risky endeavors, but required to reach the top. Remember my Pappaw said, "You'll never learn no younger". It's true. Decide right now to leave security and dare to ascend to greater things. In the end, no great business was ever created from the safety of the ground. They ascend to greatness through risk, losses, wins, and a conscience decision to climb.

2. Choose each limb carefully. Each limb is important in the climb. Some will provide you with great progress upward. Some only a little movement. But all are important. Take each one slowly. Place your foot close to the trunk of the tree where the branch is strongest. Sometimes, the branch will break. That is why climbing involves both hands and feet. Make sure the branch your hand is holding can support you when and if the branches below break. A wise decision made moments before may keep you from falling, when a bad decision causes a different branch to break. In business, decisions are thrust upon you almost moment by moment. The luxury of time to decide is not always ours. Let wisdom win the day and the serving of others be the rudder on your ship and your ascent will most often continue.

3. Check on the others. Call out to those climbing with you. "Are you okay?" "Where are you now?" "Hey... you okay?" If you hear a familiar snap and it's not coming from under you, make sure everyone else is still in the tree. Take responsibility for the others climbing with you. Coach them along the way. Stop telling people about your success. *Teach* them how to climb.

4. There is more at the top than a great view. When you get up there, soak it all in. Remember those who planted that tree when it was a seed. Take a minute to be grateful that you are alive in this moment. Shout over to the other ones who are up there with you. Point out things across the miles that they may not be seeing. Laugh. Smile. You may see loved ones from up there. Folks who's climbing days have been long past. Call their names. They will hear you and find joy in yours.

5. Listen to the voices. The wind is singing. Creation is singing. Listen. They are wise. They have a lot to teach you. The noise of this generation is deafening. Cherish the moments above the canopy. You will likely learn more there than back on the ground.

6. The climb is scary...climb *afraid*! I remember the first feeling one experiences when poking your head above the treetops is just how small we are. Let the vastness of your experience remind you that we are a small part of a bigger picture. So many are taking their treetop experience and allowing it to make them bigger than they really are. As if *they* had been there all along and not the tree. We are all important in this journey. Don't let it go to your head. Go back down and take someone up with you and keep doing that as many times as you have strength and days. That is the prize. Serving people. Our success will never rise above our own ability to cultivate that same success in others.

7. The only thing *fast* in climbing is falling back down. The biggest mistakes happen when speed is chosen over wisdom. There are those who will tell you how to be a success overnight. How to leave all the "work" behind. Just click your heels twice and money will fall from the sky. I can tell you for a fact, that the descent happens much faster than the ascent. The ground is not the goal. The canopy is the goal. Always be ascending. And when you do need to descend...do so to bring someone up with you.

I will climb to the heights once more. I will tree surf again. Who knows....you may be there with me. I sure hope so. I will never get over those moments...and hopefully...neither will you.

Coming Soon

FROM GARY GALE NORRIS

TALK TO ME:
THE UNSTOPPABLE POWER OF CONVERSATIONAL SALES

COMING SPRING 2017

And Introducing...

BUSTED KNUCKLES UNIVERSITY

ONLINE ENTREPRENEURIAL COURSES

FOLLOW GARY GALE ON FACEBOOK, TWITTER, PERISCOPE

WWW.NORRISVENTURES.COM

www.ingramcontent.com/pod-product-compliance
Lightning Source LLC
Chambersburg PA
CBHW061446180526
45170CB00004B/1577